BORN AGAIN IN CHRIST

First Steps of Faith with Jesus

STEPHEN E. CANUP

ACKNOWLEDGEMENTS

Most of the chapters in this book are extracted directly from *Knowing Jesus Intimately: A Relationship of Love-motivated, Spirit-empowered Obedience* by Stephen E. Canup. Preview this and other books at www.stephencanup.com

I sincerely appreciate David Allison for his suggestion to produce this book. As a friend and fellow prison minister, his encouragement, support and sponsorship are invaluable to me.

Everyone needs a mature spiritual mentor and trusted accountability partner. I love and appreciate Don Castleberry for fulfilling this role for me. His trust, time and commitment to me have been invaluable. He has become one of my very best friends. Don is the founder of Freedom in Jesus Prison Ministries. www.fijm.org

Special thanks to Chris Manley for cover design, copy editing and layout & design assistance. For inquiries about her work, you may contact chris@camlargraphics.com.

Appreciation is also expressed for printing and shipping services through Perfection Press. For information contact Robert Riggs, rriggs@printedtoperfection.com

Copyright 2024© by Stephen Canup. All rights reserved.

All Scripture quotations, unless otherwise indicated, are taken from the Holy Bible, New International Version®, NIV®. Copyright ©1973, 1978, 1984, 2011 by Biblica, Inc.™ Used by permission of Zondervan. All rights reserved worldwide. www.zondervan.com. The "NIV" and "New International Version" are trademarks registered in the United States Patent and Trademark Office by Biblica, Inc.™

Scripture quotations marked (AMPCE) are taken from the Amplified Bible, Copyright © 1954, 1958, 1962, 1964, 1965, 1987 by The Lockman Foundation. Used by permission.

TABLE OF CONTENTS

INTRODUCTION 1

WHAT IS THE NEW BIRTH? 3

GOD'S FORGIVENESS OF US 11

TRUE REPENTANCE 17

THE GOSPEL OF JESUS CHRIST 23

JESUS IS THE ONLY WAY 31

HOLY SPIRIT EMPOWERMENT 35

SURRENDER AND SUBMISSION 41

PRINCIPLES OF OBEDIENCE 47

TRANSFORMATION ILLUSTRATION 53

    The "Old Man" 54

    The "New Man" 56

TAKE ACTION 59

    You Can Have "The Real Thing" 61

    You Can Receive the Baptism in the Holy Spirit 63

    Water Baptism 65

    I Challenge You!!! .67

INTRODUCTION

There are no coincidences with God – only miracles for which God chooses to remain anonymous.

Since this booklet has somehow found its way to you, I believe the power of the Holy Spirit is present with you right this very minute. It might be that you have recently made a decision to follow Jesus. Or, possibly, you are seeking direction, truth and meaning; and once heard that Jesus said, "I am the way, the truth and the life…" Maybe you have questions about some of the basics of the Christian faith?

Whatever the reason you are reading this, ask the Holy Spirit to show you what He wants you to learn and do with the material that follows. He is our Helper, Teacher, Counselor, Guide and Friend. You can trust Him. Ask Him to give you spiritual eyes, and a listening, receptive heart of discernment.

When Nicodemus, a prominent leader and teacher of the Jews, came to Jesus to inquire of Him privately, Jesus told him that he must be born again to see and enter the Kingdom of God. Startled and surprised by this, Nicodemus asked, "How can this be?"

Born again? New birth? How can this be? Let's find out…

WHAT IS THE NEW BIRTH?

Many times in my life before truly surrendering to Jesus Christ – in numerous times of trouble, depression, or distress – I prayed various "prayers of salvation" but nothing really changed. I wanted something different but nothing I ever tried worked. I did not realize that I could not "change" me. Now I know that this "changing" is a work of God the Holy Spirit, and that my responsibility was to seek Him with all my heart and to be willing to submit, surrender, and be obedient to His promptings. Once I did, He began His work to re-make me into an entirely new creation.

I had heard the term "born again" but I did not really understand it, and until 2009 on a prison bunk, certainly never experienced it. What is "the new birth," and what does it mean to be "born of the Spirit?" From the website of GotQuestions.org, in May, 2024, I obtained the following answers:

Question: 'What is the new birth?'

"**Answer:** Jesus discussed the new birth in His conversation with Nicodemus, a Jewish leader, in John 3. Jesus said to him, 'Very truly I tell you, no one can see the kingdom of God unless they are born again' (John 3:3). Nicodemus was puzzled and asked how anyone could re-enter his mother's womb and be born a second time. Jesus doubled down: 'Very truly I tell you, no one can enter the kingdom of God unless they are born of water and the Spirit' (verse 5). Then He expounded on what the new birth is.

' Jesus explained that this new birth is not physical, but spiritual. The new birth that we must experience in order to 'see the kingdom of God' is a work of the Holy Spirit. Just as a mother does all the work in physical birth, so the Holy Spirit does all the work in the new birth. Upon our faith in the saving power of Jesus Christ, the Holy Spirit enters our spirits, regenerates us, and begins His work of transforming us into the image of Christ (2 Corinthians 5:17). We are born again.

"We are all born with a sin nature that separates us from our Creator. We were designed in His own image (Genesis 1:27), but that image was tarnished when we fell into sin. As sinners, we cannot fellowship with a holy God the way we are. We cannot be repaired, restored, or rehabilitated. We need to be reborn.

"In answer to Nicodemus's questions about the new birth, Jesus began talking about the wind: 'Very truly I tell you, no one can enter the kingdom of God unless they are born of water and the Spirit. Flesh gives birth to flesh, but the Spirit gives birth to spirit. You should not be surprised at my saying, 'You must be born again.' The wind blows wherever it pleases. You hear its sound, but you cannot tell where it comes from or where it is going. So it is with everyone born of the Spirit' (John 3:5-8).

"In His analogy of the wind in John 3:8, Jesus was comparing physical birth and growth with spiritual birth and growth. Jesus points out that Nicodemus need not marvel at the necessity of the Spirit causing one to be 'born again.' Nicodemus naturally believed in other things just as difficult to understand, such as the wind, which he could not see. The effects of the wind are obvious: the sound is heard, and things move as it moves. The wind, unseen, unpredictable, and uncontrollable, is mysterious to us, but we see and understand its effects. So it is with the Spirit. We do not see the Spirit, but we see the changes the Spirit produces in people. Sinful people are made holy; liars speak truth; the proud become humble. When we see such changes, we know they have a cause. The Spirit affects us just as the wind affects the trees, water, and clouds. We don't see the cause, and we don't understand all the in's and out's of how it works, but we see the effect and believe.

"When an infant is born, he continues to grow and change. A year later, two years later, ten years later, the child has changed. He does not remain an infant because a live birth results in growth. We may not see this growth happening, but we see the changes it produces. So it is with the new birth. When a person is born again in spirit, he or she is born into the family of God 'like newborn babies' (1 Peter 2:2). This birth is not visible, but it begins to produce changes that are evident.

The following are some changes that result from the new birth:

"**1. The 'fruit of the Spirit' (Galatians 5:22-23).** Someone who has experienced the new birth will begin to exhibit character qualities that are more like Jesus. This doesn't happen overnight, but just as a fruit tree grows and begins to produce fruit in season, we begin to produce godly character traits such as love, joy, peace, patience, gentleness, kindness, goodness, faithfulness, and self-control. These traits are the natural result of yielding to the Spirit and spending time with God in His Word, with His people, and in worship.

"**2. Godly choices.** Sins that once captivated us begin to fall away as we grow closer to Jesus. Our new birth broke the power that sin had over us and enables us to live in freedom. Romans 6 explains that we have died to our old way of life and are free to live as we were designed to live. Colossians 3:5 says, 'Put to death, therefore, the components of your earthly nature: sexual immorality, impurity, lust, evil desires, and greed, which is idolatry' (cf. 1 Peter 4:1). This death to sin is an ongoing process as we grow in our faith and love for the Lord.

"**3. Love for other Christians.** One of the changes the new birth produces is love: 'We love because he first loved us. Whoever claims to love God yet hates a brother or sister is a liar. For whoever does not love their brother and sister, whom they have seen, cannot love God, whom they have not seen. And he has given us this command: Anyone who loves God must also love their brother and sister' (1 John 4:19-21). A person who has been born into the family of God craves fellowship with other believers. God did not create a team where players can be traded. He did not create a corporation where employees can be fired. He created a family where every member is valued and equally loved. As part of His family, those who've been born again are to love and appreciate the other members of this worldwide family.

"**4. Spiritual gifts.** A part of God's welcome package to those who are born of His Spirit are spiritual gifts that we can use to serve Him and edify the church. Spiritual gifts are special abilities that enable us to be more effective in the particular callings God places on our lives. As each member uses his or her gifts for the good of all, God's family thrives.

"New babies crave milk, and, without it, they won't grow. Likewise, new Christians crave biblical teaching or they won't grow. Peter wrote, 'Like newborn babies, crave pure spiritual milk, so that by it you may grow up in your salvation, now that you have tasted that the Lord is good.' The new birth is only the beginning of the life God designed for us. It is also the only way we can enter the family of God and receive the privilege of calling Him 'Father' (see Matthew 6:9; Romans 8:15)."

Question:
'What does it mean to be born of the Spirit?'

"**Answer:** The Bible uses several metaphors involving birth to help explain what it means to have a saving relationship with Jesus. We find terms such as *born again* (John 3:3), *born of God* (John 1:13), and *born of the Spirit* (John 3:6). They all mean the same thing. Birth metaphors are used because we all understand physical birth. When a baby is born, a new person emerges into the world. The new life will grow, and the young person will come to resemble his or her parents. When we are born of the Spirit, a 'new person' arrives with a new spiritual life. And as we grow, we come to resemble our Father in heaven (Romans 8:29).

"People try to know God through a variety of means: some try religion or following an ethical code; some turn to intellect or logic; others try to find God in nature; and others through emotional experiences, believing that God inhabits whatever feelings they can muster when they think about Him. None of those bring us one step closer to actually communing with the God of the Bible because He cannot be known through our moral codes, our minds, our environment, or our emotions. He is Spirit, and those who would worship must worship 'in spirit and in truth' (John 4:24).

"Imagine trying to paint a portrait using a hammer and nails or trying to bake a meal using pen and paper. It would not help to try harder or cry over it because both tasks are impossible given the tools mentioned. So it is with the flesh and the Spirit. We cannot commune with a holy, incorporeal Being using sinful, fleshly means. Unless our spirits are reborn with life from God's Spirit, we simply do not have the capability to fellowship with Him. We must be born of the Spirit.

"God has instituted a way for fallen human beings to enter His holy presence, and it is the only way we can come to Him. Jesus said, 'I am the way, the truth, and the life. No one comes to the Father except through me' (John 14:6). When Jesus offered Himself as a sacrifice for sin (John 10:18) and rose again, He opened a door that had been locked. When He died on the cross, the veil of the temple was torn in two, symbolizing the fact that He has made a way to enter God's presence. God has opened the door to heaven so that whoever trusts in His Son's sacrifice can be born again in his or her spirit (Mark 15:38).

"When we place our faith in the risen Christ, a divine transaction takes place (2 Corinthians 5:21). God removes from us the sin, guilt, and condemnation we deserve because of our rebellion against Him. He throws our sin as far as the east is from the west (Psalm 103:12). At the moment of repentance and faith, the Holy Spirit breathes new life into us, and our bodies become His temple (1 Corinthians 3:16). Our spirits can now commune with God's Spirit as He assures us that we belong to Him (Romans 8:16).

"We might think of the human spirit like a deflated balloon that hangs lifeless inside our hearts. We are scarcely aware of its existence until God calls our names and an awakening begins. When we respond to God's call with repentance and faith in what Jesus Christ has done for our salvation, we are born of the Spirit. At that point the balloon inflates. The Holy Spirit moves into our spirits and fills us. He begins His transforming work so that we begin to resemble Jesus (2 Corinthians 5:17; Romans 8:29).

"There are only two types of people in the world: those who are born of the Spirit and those who are not. In the end, only those two categories matter (John 3:3). Our earthly lives are extended opportunities for us to respond to God's call and become born of the Spirit (Hebrews 3:15)."

In my own experience, I am continually amazed at the changes the Holy Spirit is making in my life as He progressively sanctifies me, conforming me a little more every day closer to the image of Jesus. I am overwhelmed when I stop to consider how much the Father loves me and longs to be in relationship with me. Being truly "born again" is the very best thing that has ever happened to me!

Some Relevant Scripture Passages

John 3:3-9 "Jesus replied, 'Very truly I tell you, no one can see the kingdom of God unless they are born again.' 'How can someone be born when they are old?' Nicodemus asked. 'Surely they cannot enter a second time into their mother's womb to be born ' Jesus answered, 'Very truly I tell you, no one can enter the kingdom of God unless they are born of water and the Spirit. Flesh gives birth to flesh, but the Spirit gives birth to spirit. You should not be surprised at my saying, 'You must be born again.' The wind blows wherever it pleases. You hear its sound, but you cannot tell where it comes from or where it is going. So it is with everyone born of the Spirit.' 'How can this be?' Nicodemus asked."

2 Corinthians 5:17 "Therefore, if anyone is in Christ, the new creation has come: The old has gone, the new is here!"

1 Peter 2:2-3 "Like newborn babies, crave pure spiritual milk, so that by it you may grow up in your salvation, now that you have tasted that the Lord is good."

Galatians 5:22-23 "But the fruit of the Spirit is love joy, peace, forbearance, kindness, goodness, faithfulness, gentleness and self-control. Against such things there is no law."

1 John 4:19-21 "We love because he first loved us. Whoever claims to love God yet hates a brother or sister is a liar. For whoever does not love their brother and sister, whom they have seen, cannot love God, whom they have not seen. And he has given us this command: Anyone who loves God must also love their brother and sister."

Romans 8:15 "The Spirit you received does not make you slaves, so that you live in fear again; rather, the Spirit you received brought about your adoption to sonship. And by him we cry, 'Abba, Father.'"

John 1:12-13 "Yet to all who did receive him, to those who believed in his name, he gave the right to become children of God — children born not of natural descent, nor of human decision or a husband's will, but born of God."

Romans 8:29 "For those God foreknew he also predestined to be conformed to the image of his Son, that he might be the firstborn among many brothers and sisters."

John 14:6 "Jesus answered, 'I am the way and the truth and the life. No one comes to the Father except through me.'"

John 4:24 "God is spirit, and his worshipers must worship in the Spirit and in truth."

2 Corinthians 5:21 "God made him who had no sin to be sin for us, so that in him we might become the righteousness of God."

Takeaway Highlight

"We are all born with a sin nature that separates us from our Creator. We were designed in His own image (Genesis 1:27), but that image was tarnished when we fell into sin. As sinners, we cannot fellowship with a holy God the way we are. We cannot be repaired, restored, or rehabilitated. We need to be reborn."

Practical Application

Spend a few minutes thinking that it is actually possible to have a totally new start in life. All your past can be washed away. Old wounds can be healed. Sins can be forgiven.

True intimacy of relationship begins when we believe, and receive the incredible grace of God's forgiveness for all our sins. It seems almost too good to be true.

Let's learn more about this incredible truth...

GOD'S FORGIVENESS OF US

Our relationship with God begins when we believe, truly repent, receive God's forgiveness, then turn from our old way of life. Surely, all of us know we need plenty of forgiveness! Amen?

I was saved as a young boy in a Baptist church where my family attended. However, for most of my life I did not attend church or make any serious attempt to follow Jesus. If you have ever read my testimony, you will remember that I sinned more and more, indulged in many addictions, and descended into depravity after God turned me over to my own desires and reprobation. I was guilty of almost everything Paul describes about this condition in Romans 1:21-32. Eventually my sin landed me in prison with a six-year sentence.

Having been in an emotional and mental state of severe and frequently suicidal depression for years, I believed for the longest time the lie of the enemy that there was no hope of anything ever getting better. Additionally, I believed his lie that I had gone too far and done too much for God to forgive me. I was overcome with guilt, regret, remorse and shame. Have you felt this way?

In their booklet on "The Forgiveness of God," RBC Ministries says, "If we believe our emotions, we may feel we have gone too far. Our self-contempt seems deserved. But there's hope. God wants us to believe in His ability to forgive sins we cannot forget. God is angry at sin, but His anger is not a denial of His love...The truth is that His love is equal to His anger, and because of His love He found a way to show mercy. He sent His Son Jesus.

"God's justice – which demanded punishment for sinners – was satisfied by Jesus. The payment for our sin came at Heaven's expense... God built a two-lane bridge of mercy and justice over the chasm of

BORN AGAIN IN CHRIST | 11

sin separating us and Him. When Jesus was crucified, God accepted the sacrifice as sufficient payment for our sin. Justice was satisfied... Three days later, Christ rose bodily from the dead. By the miracle of the resurrection He showed Heaven's acceptance of His sacrifice.

"Our sin was forgiven. Our guilt was removed. By one man, once and for all! Because of the unlimited scope of Christ's death on the cross, we have received forgiveness not only for past sins, but for all sins – past, present, and future...The moment we trust Christ as Savior, we are given immunity from punishment. The issue is settled: Our case is closed and God will not open the files of our guilt again. Just as the courts of earth honor the principle of double jeopardy, heaven will not judge twice those whose sins have been punished in Christ. We will not be tried again for the sins He bore in our place."

Jesus was made by the Father to be sin with our sinfulness, so that we could be made righteous with His righteousness. What a beautiful exchange (2 Corinthians 5:21)! God declares as righteous all those who appeal to the death of Christ as payment for their sin. No sin is excluded. We are saved by faith alone in Christ alone. There is nothing in the entire universe more powerful than the Blood of Jesus that takes away our sin. When we do not deny the Spirit – and thereby accept by faith what Jesus did for us – there is no sin (and no sinner) beyond God's love and forgiveness.

In an article entitled, "The Forgiveness of our Sins." by Dr. Charles Stanley wrote, "Based on the authority of the Bible, I can tell you without reservation that God loves you, and He forgives everyone who trusts Christ as Savior. Scripture says:

• With His blood, Jesus paid our entire sin debt and obtained our full pardon (Matt. 26:28). Every sin – without exception – is covered (Col. 2:13-14).

• Forgiveness is given to everyone who believes in Jesus (Acts 10:43) and remains available to all believers (1 John 1:9).

• Our pardon for sin is based on the riches of our Father's grace, which always exceeds the offense (Eph. 1:7; Rom. 5:20).

- God doesn't count past, present, or future sins against us (Rom. 8:1; 2 Cor. 5:19).

"To reconcile us to Himself, God sent His Son to die in our place. He accepted Christ's sacrifice as payment in full for our transgressions. He offers forgiveness solely on the basis of our relationship with Jesus, not on our behavior. Because of our faith in Christ's completed work on the cross, we can be assured that we have received and will continue to receive His divine mercy.

"Scripture assures us that no transgression is beyond the scope of God's pardon. This isn't license to sin – far from it! Divine forgiveness should instead motivate a passion for holiness. If you're struggling to accept God's forgiveness, reread the verses above, and be thankful for such a great gift."

The Bible is filled with declarations of God's love and forgiveness. Your sins are not excluded. This was a major realization for me. I knew I could start over. I found present and eternal hope, and freedom, in Jesus! Receive God's forgiveness.

Some Relevant Scripture Passages

I John 1:9 "If we confess our sins, he is faithful and just and will forgive us our sins and purify us from all unrighteousness."

II Chronicles 7:14 "...if my people, who are called by my name, will humble themselves and pray and seek my face and turn from their wicked ways, then will I hear from heaven and will forgive their sin and will heal their land."

Colossians 2:13 "When you were dead in your sins and in the uncircumcision of your sinful nature, God made you alive with Christ. He forgave us all our sins..."

Psalm 103:11-12 "For as high as the heavens are above the earth, so great is his love for those who fear him; as far as the east is from the west, so far has he removed our transgressions from us."

Micah 7:18-19 "Who is a God like you, who pardons sin and forgives the transgression of the remnant of his inheritance? You do not stay angry forever but delight to show mercy. You will again have compassion on us; you will tread our sins underfoot and hurl all our iniquities into the depths of the sea."

Psalm 32:1-5 "Blessed is he whose transgressions are forgiven, whose sins are covered. Blessed is the man whose sin the LORD does not count against him and in whose spirit is no deceit. When I kept silent, my bones wasted away through my groaning all day long. For day and night your hand was heavy upon me; my strength was sapped as in the heat of summer. Then I acknowledged my sin to you and did not cover up my iniquity. I said, 'I will confess my transgressions to the LORD' – and you forgave the guilt of my sin."

Other passages: John 3:16; Psalm 130:3-4; Psalm 86:5; Proverbs 28:13; Jeremiah 31:34; Isaiah 44:22; Isaiah 55:6-7.

Takeaway Highlight

The Bible is filled with declarations of God's love and forgiveness. Your sins are not excluded. Our relationship with God begins when we believe and receive God's forgiveness of us, and truly repent by turning from our old way of life.

Practical Application

Think about how many examples are provided in the Bible of sinners that God forgave. Do you sometimes wonder if God can really forgive and utilize you? Look what He did for others:

Adam and Eve - The first humans to sin also became the first to experience God's forgiveness (Gen. 3).

Moses - Although he murdered an Egyptian in anger, God chose him to deliver His people from slavery; to take them to the promised land; to spend time personally in God's presence; and, to become known as a "friend of God" (Ex. 2,3,33,34).

Aaron - Although he was involved in making a golden calf, Aaron later was head of the priesthood (Ex. 32; Lev. 8).

Aaron and Miriam - When they opposed Moses' God-given authority, Miriam was stricken with leprosy. But they confessed and were forgiven and cleansed (Num. 12).

Eliphaz, Bildad, Zophar - These men falsely accused Job and misrepresented God, but they were forgiven (Job 42).

Rahab - This Jericho prostitute turned to the Lord of Israel and became part of Jesus' family tree (Josh. 2; Matt. 1:5).

David - Although he was guilty of murder and adultery, David repented and confessed his sin. He was spoken of as a man after God's own heart (II Sam. 11-12; Ps. 51).

Matthew - This tax collector with a bad reputation became Christ's disciple (Matt. 9:9-13).

A Criminal - When he cried out to Jesus on the cross, this thief was welcomed into paradise (Lk. 23:40-43).

Peter - Though he denied Christ three times, Peter became a pillar in the church (Mk. 14:66-72; Jn. 21:15-19).

A Woman Caught in Adultery - Her accusers backed away and Christ forgave her sins (John 8:1-11).

Paul - Killer of Christians and self-confessed "chief of sinners." Paul is a prime example of the grace of God (Acts 9; I Tim. 1:15).

Corinthian Believers - Once they were idolaters, adulterers, homosexuals, thieves, greedy, slanderers, and swindlers, but then they experienced God's forgiveness (I Cor. 6:9-11).

Spend a few minutes re-reading these examples. God can still utilize you. He has a plan for your life. What He did for others, He will do for you!!!

An intimate relationship with Jesus starts the minute we truly repent, surrender, believe the Gospel, and are born again. Have you ever truly repented and turned from your lifestyle of sin?

TRUE REPENTANCE

The Bible is very clear that true repentance is required for effective salvation. There are many scriptures in both the Old and New Testaments stressing the importance of true repentance. The Bible says to "Repent, and believe the Gospel"; "Repent, and be saved"; and, "Repent, and be baptized." Are you certain that you have come to salvation by way of true repentance?

A decision to accept Jesus as Savior is not effective if it does not lead to a change of direction – away from sin, towards God. Repentance is not an emotion – for example, not the feeling of "I am sorry." or, "I feel bad about what I've done" – rather, it is a decision. It is like deciding to make a "U-turn" on a highway. You are then headed in the opposite direction from where you were going. Someone in true repentance does not just say "I'm sorry I did that"; they will also live a different life demonstrating a new mind-set of "I won't do it again."

The Greek words translated as "repentance" in the New Testament mean "to think differently," "a reversal of a decision," "to change your mind," "to turn about in opinion," "to turn about from an intended way," and to change "attitudes, thoughts and behaviors concerning the demands of God for right living," Similarly, Webster's dictionary defines "repent" as "to turn from sin and resolve to reform one's life."

There are over 70 scriptures about repentance. Some of them include: Psalm 51:17; Matthew 3:1-2, 11; Matthew 4:17; Mark 1:4, 14-15; Mark 6 12; Luke 5:32; Luke 15:7; Acts 2:38; Acts 3:19; Acts 11:18; II Corinthians 7 9-10; II Timothy 2:25; II Peter 3:9; and, Revelation 3:19.

True repentance is not just a change of mind. It is also a change of attitude and heart. It involves a Godly sorrow and regret because of personal sin, and results in a radical break with sin. J.C. Ryle said "The beginning of the way to Heaven is to feel that we are on the way to hell." Dr. Charles Stanley said, "An unrepentant man or woman is not condemned by God (to hell), rather has chosen to remain in the company of all those condemned by their own free will."

In the Old Testament, Psalm 51, David gives us a great example of an attitude of true repentance. He has a "broken spirit and contrite heart" (Psalm 51:17) over his actions of adultery and murder surrounding his affair with Bathsheba. David knew he could not come to God with his own self-righteousness; rather, he approached God with a broken heart and a spirit willing to change. Lydia Reimer writes, "Repentance tears down the wall of separation that stands between us and God. It prepares us for His presence." Be sure to read all of Psalm 51 carefully to get a more complete understanding of David's exemplary approach to repentance.

The parable about the prodigal son in Luke 15:11-24, is one of best teachings of Jesus that illustrates the kind of repentance it takes to go home to the Father. The "U-turn" occurs in verse 17 where it says "he came to himself," or "he came to his senses." He made a decision to turn around and go home. Then he took action by getting up out of his mess and actually going along the road home – in a different direction than when he left home earlier when "he set off for a distant country and there squandered his wealth in wild living" (Luke 15:13).

Bible teacher R.B. Thieme, Jr. writes, "What does it mean to come to yourself? It means to look at life from the biblical perspective: to face up to the situation as it really exists; to recognize the sins in your own life; to stop rationalizing or justifying your sins; to stop blaming God or someone else (operation patsy) and to actually acknowledge your sin – to recognize that you are wrong and contrary to the Word of God."

In Mere Christianity, author C.S. Lewis is describing the "hole" in which we find ourselves before we come to our senses like the prodigal son. "Now what sort of 'hole' had (he) gotten himself into? He had tried to set up on his own, to behave as if he belonged to himself.

In other words, fallen man is not simply an imperfect creature who needs improvement: he is a rebel who must lay down his arms. Laying down your arms, surrendering, saying you are sorry, realizing that you have been on the wrong track and getting ready to start life all over again from the ground floor – that is the only way out of our 'hole'. This process of surrender – this movement full speed astern (in the opposite direction) – is what Christians call repentance."

In summary, "true repentance" involves a real change of heart, leading to a complete change of mind, which in turn leads to a change of direction – away from sin and toward the Father. It is like making a U-turn when you are going the wrong way down a one-way street. You realize in your mind that you are headed the wrong way, and you have a change of heart that makes you want to turn completely around to go in the opposite but correct direction. There will be visible evidence of the change, and you will resolve not to turn back around the wrong way.

In our new direction, if we temporarily stumble, we do not let the enemy's lies convince us to turn permanently back to our old direction. Instead, we quickly confess our sin (1 John 1:9), and we allow the Holy Spirit to empower and encourage us to get up and continue on the right path towards the Father. True repentance has evidence of a permanently changed direction, and a significantly changed life.

If you ever prayed a prayer of salvation before but nothing ever changed about the direction of your life, I strongly suggest to you that you did not repent. If you did not repent, you were not saved! God heard your words but He read your heart. If you were not ready to turn from your old way of living and do your best to follow Jesus, then you did not repent. In your mind you may have wanted the benefits of salvation, but in your heart you were not really willing to allow Jesus to be the Lord of your life.

Has true repentance changed your direction? Have you made a 'U-turn"? If not, please "run to God with repentance in one hand and praise in the other" (Tommy Tenney). Like me, you will be glad you did!!!

Some Relevant Scripture Passages

Isaiah 30:15 "For thus the Lord God, the Holy One of Israel, has said, 'In repentance and rest you will be saved, in quietness and trust is your strength.'"

Acts 3:19 "Therefore repent and return, so that your sins may be wiped away, in order that times of refreshing may come from the presence of the Lord."

Romans 2:4 "Do you think lightly of the riches of His kindness and tolerance and patience, not knowing that the kindness of God leads you to repentance?"

James 4:8 "Draw near to God and He will draw near to you. Cleanse your hands, you sinners; and purify your hearts, you double-minded."

1 John 1:9 "If we confess our sins, He is faithful and righteous to forgive us our sins and to cleanse us from all unrighteousness."

Luke 5:32 "I have not come to call the righteous but sinners to repentance."

Luke 15:7 "I tell you that in the same way, there will be more joy in heaven over one sinner who repents than over ninety-nine righteous persons who need no repentance."

Luke 24:47 "Repentance for forgiveness of sins would be proclaimed in His name to all the nations, beginning from Jerusalem."

2 Corinthians 7:9-10 "I now rejoice, not that you were made sorrowful, but that you were made sorrowful to the point of repentance; for you were made sorrowful according to the will of God, so that you might not suffer loss in anything through us. For the sorrow that is according to the will of God produces a repentance without regret, leading to salvation, but the sorrow of the world produces death."

2 Peter 3:9 "The Lord is not slow about His promise, as some count slowness, but is patient toward you, not wishing for any to perish but for all to come to repentance."

Mark 1:15 "The time is fulfilled, and the kingdom of God is at hand; repent and believe in the gospel."

Ezekiel 18: 21-22 "If the wicked man turns from all his sins which he has committed and observes all My statutes and practices justice and righteousness, he shall surely live; he shall not die. All his transgressions which he has committed will not be remembered against him; because of his righteousness which he has practiced, he will live."

Takeaway Highlight

True repentance involves a real change of heart, leading to a complete change of mind, which in turn leads to a change of direction – away from sin and toward the Father. In our new direction, if we temporarily stumble, we do not let the enemy's lies convince us to turn permanently back to our old direction. Instead, we quickly confess our sin (1 John 1:9), and we allow the Holy Spirit to empower and encourage us to get up and continue on the right path towards the Father. True repentance results in a permanently changed direction, and a significantly changed life.

Practical Application

Take some quiet time to consider if you have truly repented of your old ways. Are you cooperating with the Holy Spirit as He leads you daily on the right path? Was there ever a time when you were truly sorrowful for your sin and told God about it? Did you change your direction away from sin to determinedly walk towards God? When you stumble do you get up quickly, repent and keep heading the right direction?

An intimate relationship with Jesus starts the minute we truly repent, surrender, believe the Gospel, and are born again. Have you believed the Gospel of Jesus Christ and been born again?

THE GOSPEL OF JESUS CHRIST

The Apostle Paul, in Romans 1:16, wrote, "For I am not ashamed of the gospel, because it is the power of God that brings salvation to everyone who believes: first to the Jew, then to the Gentile."

But what exactly is the gospel to which Paul is referring?

It is the Gospel of Jesus Christ. I found a good summary at www.GotQuestions.org which I present here in the following five paragraphs:

"The word *gospel* means 'good news,' so the gospel of Christ is the good news of His coming to provide forgiveness of sins for all who will believe (Colossians 1:14; Romans 10:9). Since the first man's sin, mankind has been under the condemnation of God (Romans 5:12). Because everyone breaks God's perfect law by committing sin, everyone is guilty (Romans 3:23). The punishment for the crime of sin is physical death (Romans 6:23) and then an eternity spent in a place of punishment (Revelation 20:15; Matthew 25:46). This eternal separation from God is also called the "second death" (Revelation 20:14-15).

"The bad news that all are guilty of sin and condemned by God is countered by the gospel, the good news of Jesus Christ. God, because of His love for the world, has made a way for man to be forgiven of their sins (John 3:16). He sent His Son, Jesus Christ, to take the sins of mankind on Himself through death on a cross (1 Peter 2:24). In placing our sin on Christ, God ensured that all who will believe in the name of Jesus will be forgiven (Acts 10:43). Jesus' resurrection guarantees the justification of all who believe (Romans 4:25).

"The Bible specifies the content of the gospel message: 'Now, brothers and sisters, I want to remind you of the gospel I preached to you, which you received and on which you have taken your stand. By this gospel you are saved, if you hold firmly to the word I preached to you. Otherwise, you have believed in vain. For what I received I passed on to you as of first importance: that Christ died for our sins according to the Scriptures, that he was buried, that he was raised on the third day according to the Scriptures, and that he appeared to Cephas, and then to the Twelve. After that, he appeared to more than five hundred of the brothers and sisters at the same time' (1 Corinthians 15:1-6). In this passage, Paul emphasizes the primacy of the gospel – it is of 'first importance.' The gospel message contains two historical facts, both supported by Scripture: Christ's death and His resurrection. Both those facts are bolstered by other proofs: Christ's death is proved by His burial, and His resurrection is proved by the eyewitnesses.

"The gospel of Jesus Christ is the good news that God provided the way for man to be freed from the penalty of sin (John 14:6; Romans 6:23). Everyone dies physically, but those who believe in Jesus Christ are promised a physical resurrection unto eternal life (John 11:23-26). Those who reject Christ will not only die physically but will undergo a 'second death,' which the Bible describes as an eternal lake of fire (Revelation 20:13-14). Jesus is the only One in whom salvation can be found (Acts 4:12).

"The gospel of Jesus Christ is the best news anyone will ever hear, and what a person does with this news will determine where he or she spends eternity. God is calling you to choose life. Call on the name of the Lord and be saved (Romans 10:13)."

From a tract, "What is the Gospel," Greg Gilbert explains in the following three paragraphs what our response should be to hearing the Gospel:

"What does God expect us to do with the information that Jesus died in our place so we can be saved from God's righteous wrath against our sins? He expects us to respond with repentance and faith.

"To repent of our sins means to turn away from our rebellion against God. Repentance doesn't mean we'll bring an immediate end to our sinning. It does mean, though, that we'll never again live at peace with our sins.

"Not only that, but we also turn to God in faith. Faith is reliance. It's a promise-founded trust in the risen Jesus to save you from your sins. If God is ever to count us righteous, he'll have to do it on the basis of someone else's record, someone who's qualified to stand in as our substitute. And that's what happens when a person is saved by Jesus: All our sins are credited to Jesus who took the punishment for them, and the perfect righteousness of Jesus is then credited to us when we place our trust in what he has done for us! That's what faith means – to rely on Jesus, to trust in him alone to stand in our place and win a righteous verdict from God!"

Because of the times, it is so very important that those of us who are true believers let our lights shine in the midst of ever-increasing darkness. We must be salt that flavors and preserves. As chaos increases, our peace, calm and joy in the middle of the storm will draw unbelievers to come to us and ask how they can have what we possess in Christ Jesus. Let the reality and sincerity of your genuine faith be evident to all in the way you live daily. Actions speak louder than words.

The purpose of knowing the Gospel of Jesus Christ is so that you are better equipped with the tools you need to explain your eternal life and hope in Jesus to others. It should also solidify your confidence in your own salvation as you take time to meditate on the Word of God, and especially on the unconditional, everlasting love of the Father towards you. The Gospel is more than most of us realize! The scriptures below are selected to show you and others the magnificence and wonder of His complete salvation available for those who truly believe, receive, and repent.

I encourage you to read this chapter often so you can use it to help and encourage others when they come to you. We are entering the times when Jesus said, "men's hearts would be failing them for fear of looking after those things coming upon the Earth." We must "work while it is day because night is coming when no man can work." Your prayers will become ever more powerful as you study and believe the

Word of God. Stay submitted and surrendered daily to the Lordship of Jesus and the Leadership of the Holy Spirit.

Let me strongly encourage you to realize what an outstanding opportunity God has given you to positively impact the Kingdom during the coming days. You are God's Ambassador. Ask God for more boldness to speak the Word of God (Acts 4:27-31; 5:41-42).

I pray you will personally rededicate your life to go "all in, and all out" for Jesus. Ask the Holy Spirit to set you apart from the world, and make you ever more holy daily. Make up your mind to do the best you can to be obedient in every area of your life, and repent quickly if you fall. This is absolutely not the time to be "lukewarm," "on the fence," or "playing with God."

Some Relevant Scripture Passages

As true followers of Jesus Christ, we must always be prepared to respond when someone asks us about our faith in Christ Jesus – or maybe they want to know about our peace, calm and joy in the middle of the crazy, dark days our world is experiencing. Here are a number of scriptures that, when considered together, give a clear picture of the Good News of the Gospel of Jesus Christ:

1 Peter 3:15-16 "But in your hearts revere Christ as Lord. Always be prepared to give an answer to everyone who asks you to give the reason for the hope that you have. But do this with gentleness and respect, keeping a clear conscience, so that those who speak maliciously against your good behavior in Christ may be ashamed of their slander."

John 3:16-17 "For God so loved the world that he gave his one and only Son, that whoever believes in him shall not perish but have eternal life. For God did not send his Son into the world to condemn the world, but to save the world through him."

1 Corinthians 15:1-8 "Now, brothers and sisters, I want to remind you of the gospel I preached to you, which you received and on which you have taken your stand. By this gospel you are saved, if you hold firmly to the word I preached to you. Otherwise, you have believed in vain.

"For what I received I passed on to you as of first importance: that Christ died for our sins according to the Scriptures, that he was buried, that he was raised on the third day according to the Scriptures, and that he appeared to Cephas, and then to the Twelve. After that, he appeared to more than five hundred of the brothers and sisters at the same time, most of whom are still living, though some have fallen asleep. Then he appeared to James, then to all the apostles, and last of all he appeared to me also, as to one abnormally born."

Colossians 1:15-23 "The Son is the image of the invisible God, the firstborn over all creation. For in him all things were created: things in heaven and on earth, visible and invisible, whether thrones or powers or rulers or authorities; all things have been created through him and for him. He is before all things, and in him all things hold together. And he is the head of the body, the church; he is the beginning and the firstborn from among the dead, so that in everything he might have the supremacy. For God was pleased to have all his fullness dwell in him, and through him to reconcile to himself all things, whether things on earth or things in heaven, by making peace through his blood, shed on the cross. Once you were alienated from God and were enemies in your minds because of your evil behavior. But now he has reconciled you by Christ's physical body through death to present you holy in his sight, without blemish and free from accusation – if you continue in your faith, established and firm, and do not move from the hope held out in the gospel. This is the gospel that you heard and that has been proclaimed to every creature under heaven, and of which I, Paul, have become a servant."

Philippians 2:5-11 "In your relationships with one another, have the same mindset as Christ Jesus:

Who, being in very nature God,
    did not consider equality with God something to be used to his own advantage;

rather, he made himself nothing
> by taking the very nature of a servant,
> being made in human likeness.
And being found in appearance as a man,
> he humbled himself
> by becoming obedient to death—
>> even death on a cross!

Therefore God exalted him to the highest place
> and gave him the name that is above every name,
that at the name of Jesus every knee should bow,
> in heaven and on earth and under the earth,
and every tongue acknowledge that Jesus Christ is Lord,
> to the glory of God the Father."

Acts 10:34-43 Then Peter began to speak: "I now realize how true it is that God does not show favoritism but accepts from every nation the one who fears him and does what is right. You know the message God sent to the people of Israel, announcing the good news of peace through Jesus Christ, who is Lord of all. You know what has happened throughout the province of Judea, beginning in Galilee after the baptism that John preached – how God anointed Jesus of Nazareth with the Holy Spirit and power, and how he went around doing good and healing all who were under the power of the devil, because God was with him.

"We are witnesses of everything he did in the country of the Jews and in Jerusalem. They killed him by hanging him on a cross, but God raised him from the dead on the third day and caused him to be seen. He was not seen by all the people, but by witnesses whom God had already chosen – by us who ate and drank with him after he rose from the dead. He commanded us to preach to the people and to testify that he is the one whom God appointed as judge of the living and the dead. All the prophets testify about him that everyone who believes in him receives forgiveness of sins through his name."

Acts 5:30-32 "The God of our ancestors raised Jesus from the dead – whom you killed by hanging him on a cross. God exalted him to his own right hand as Prince and Savior that he might bring Israel to repentance and forgive their sins. We are witnesses of these things, and so is the Holy Spirit, whom God has given to those who obey him."

Acts 2:22-24; 32-33 "Fellow Israelites, listen to this: Jesus of Nazareth was a man accredited by God to you by miracles, wonders and signs, which God did among you through him, as you yourselves know. This man was handed over to you by God's deliberate plan and foreknowledge; and you, with the help of wicked men, put him to death by nailing him to the cross. But God raised him from the dead, freeing him from the agony of death, because it was impossible for death to keep its hold on him... 32 God has raised this Jesus to life, and we are all witnesses of it. Exalted to the right hand of God, he has received from the Father the promised Holy Spirit and has poured out what you now see and hear."

Hebrews 1:1-3 "In the past God spoke to our ancestors through the prophets at many times and in various ways, but in these last days he has spoken to us by his Son, whom he appointed heir of all things, and through whom also he made the universe. The Son is the radiance of God's glory and the exact representation of his being, sustaining all things by his powerful word. After he had provided purification for sins, he sat down at the right hand of the Majesty in heaven."

Other important Scriptures:
John 1:1-5, 9-14; Isaiah 53;Psalm 22; Acts 8:30-35; Romans 10:9-15; Acts 13:26-39; Titus 2:11-14; Colossians 1:13-14; 2 Corinthians 5:17-21.

Takeaway Highlight

The gospel of Jesus Christ is the best news anyone will ever hear, and what a person does with this news will determine where he or she spends eternity. God is calling you to choose life. Call on the name of the Lord and be saved (Romans 10:13).

Practical Application

If you have never believed the Gospel, confessed Jesus as your Savior and Lord, repented and been "born again," and you would like to do that now, please turn to page 61. If you made this decision, congratulations!

From the scriptures presented above, write up your own simple summary of what is the Gospel of Jesus Christ. Think about this chapter deeply. Spend some time talking to God the Father about how your life has changed since you believed and received the "Good News." Ask the Holy Spirit to bring someone across your path who needs to know Jesus. Pray for specific people you know who are not yet believers to come to the point where they desire a personal relationship with Jesus.

A prevalent false belief is that there are several paths to God. Do not be deceived, Jesus is the only way to our Creator, Father God. Let's examine this truth more...

JESUS IS THE ONLY WAY

Do not be deceived; Jesus is the only way to God.

When four of Jesus' closest disciples went to Him privately to ask Him what would be the signs of His Second Coming and of the "end of the age," Jesus warned them several times not to be deceived. Surely, we are even now seeing all the signs come to pass before our very eyes just as He foretold. Likewise, we are already seeing signs of the great deception.

We believe the greatest part of this deception is to try to convince the world that there are more ways to God and Heaven than just through Jesus. THAT IS A LIE. DO NOT BE DECEIVED. The only way to Father God is through the finished work of Jesus Christ of Nazareth at the cross and through His resurrection.

Many are suggesting that Jesus is just one way to Heaven, not necessarily the only way. This has reportedly come from even a few influential leaders within "Christian" circles! It is heresy to espouse this view.

In this age of secular humanism where mankind says they determine their own fate and future, not God, we as Christians are susceptible to their attempts to convince everyone that truth is "relative" to what is going on in society, and so it changes with the times. We are urged to be tolerant of everyone for every reason. No-one must be "offended." We are told that everyone must be "included" and not "confronted" in any way about anything.

While we must certainly treat those who do not agree with us with respect, kindness and gentleness, we must be very careful not to compromise on Who we know is Truth – the Son of God, Jesus Christ.

Jesus makes it very clear that He is the only way, the only truth and the only life. He assures us that no-one gets to the Father except through Him (see John 14:6).

Peter preached about this truth about Jesus in Acts 4:12 when he said, "Salvation is found in no one else, for there is no other name under heaven given to mankind by which we must be saved." Isaiah quotes Jehovah, Father God, in Isaiah 43:11 as saying, "I, even I, am the Lord, and apart from me there is no savior."

In a devotional entitled, "Jesus: The Only Way to Heaven," Dr. Charles Stanley writes,

"While the world has many religions, there is only one way to heaven. Jesus clearly states that 'no-one comes to the father but through me' (John 14:6). To emphasize this point, He used several picturesque descriptions, calling Himself the Living Bread, the Door, the Good Shepherd, and the Way (John 6:51; 10:9-11; 14:6)."

Dr. Stanley concludes his devotional with, "Scripture declares that there is but one way to Heaven – through faith in Jesus Christ. His gospel is a straight path from the pit of sin to the Glory of Heaven, with the promise of an abundant life in between. What we must do is go through the Door and follow the Way; then the Living Bread will sustain us."

Pastor Max Lucado wrote, "As long as Jesus is one of many options and ways to heaven, He is no option at all. As long as you can carry your own burdens, you don't need a burden bearer. As long as your situation brings you no grief, you will receive no comfort. And, as long as you can take Him or leave Him you might as well leave Him because He won't be taken half-heartedly."

I urge you to study carefully what Jesus revealed in Matthew 24, Mark 13, and Luke 21. Paul gives us further insight in 1 Thessalonians 4:13 – 5:11; 2 Thessalonians 2:1-17; 1 Timothy 4:1-2; and 2 Timothy 3:1-5. Read the visions of Daniel the prophet in Daniel chapters 7, 11 and 12. Of course, John tells us about the end of the age in Revelation. After studying these passages, I am certain you will agree that surely these times in which we are living are "the last days."

Brothers and Sisters, there is a sense of urgency in me to implore you to be careful you are not deceived – Jesus Christ of Nazareth is the only way to the Father in Heaven. Ask the Father for keen discernment through His Holy Spirit to recognize and avoid the coming great deception.

Jesus is coming back for His people (John 14:1-3). He is coming quickly, in an instant of time (Matthew 24:27). Jesus is coming soon, any day now (Revelation 22:12-13). Are you sure you're ready (Matthew 24:42-44)?

Some Relevant Scripture Passages

John 14:6 Jesus said, "I am the way, the truth, and the life. No one comes to the Father except through Me."

John 11:25-26 Jesus said, "I am the resurrection and the life. He who believes in me though he may die, he shall live."

Acts 4:12 "Salvation is found in no one else, for there is no other name under heaven given to mankind by which we must be saved."

John 6:44 Jesus said, "No one can come to me unless the Father who sent me draws them, and I will raise them up at the last day."

Romans 5:8-9 "But God demonstrates his own love for us in this: While we were still sinners, Christ died for us. Since we have now been justified by his blood, how much more shall we be saved from God's wrath through him!"

Romans 6:23 "For the wages of sin is death, but the gift of God is eternal life in Christ Jesus our Lord."

Romans 10:9-10 "If you declare with your mouth, 'Jesus is Lord,' and believe in your heart that God raised him from the dead, you will be saved. For it is with your heart that you believe and are justified, and it is with your mouth that you profess your faith and are saved."

Isaiah 43:11 Jehovah said, "I, even I, am the Lord, and apart from me there is no savior."

Takeaway Highlight

"As long as Jesus is one of many options and ways to heaven, He is no option at all. As long as you can carry your own burdens, you don't need a burden bearer. As long as your situation brings you no grief, you will receive no comfort. And, as long as you can take Him or leave Him you might as well leave Him because He won't be taken half-heartedly." Max Lucado

Practical Application

Prayerfully consider this: if Jesus is not the only way, why would God the Father make Him go through arguably the cruelest form of torture and death ever invented? If He is not Who He said He was, He is a liar, or a maniac or worse, and would not be worthy of any kind of following whatsoever. Also, he would not be "a good teacher" or "a prophet." For great background on why Jesus is the Only Way, check out the writings of Josh McDowell, More than a Carpenter, and Lee Strobel's book, The Case for Christ.

When a person believes and receives salvation in Jesus as the Only Way, the Father and the Son send their Holy Spirit to live in them for empowerment...

HOLY SPIRIT EMPOWERMENT

Intimacy of relationship with the Father and the Son are available only through their Holy Spirit. Since the Holy Spirit is their gift to every believer to dwell inside them daily, we should learn all we can about the One Who is our Helper, Teacher, Counselor, Friend and Guide. True power to walk out the Christian life in love-motivated obedience is available only in and through the Holy Spirit.

The same power that raised Jesus from the dead dwells in you. The Father's power on Earth is administered only through His Holy Spirit. The creative power of God is the Holy Spirit. The Spirit of the Father, the Spirit of the Son, is not only around you, He lives in you! What a mystery, "Christ in you, the hope of Glory"! See Colossians 1:27.

R.B. Thieme, III wrote, "The Holy Spirit is the unseen power of God, the Person through whom divine power is conveyed."

When I was still incarcerated I saw several Christians who were released before me leave, only to return to prison within a year or so. I had also heard of others that were following Jesus in prison with me who, after their release, fell away from their relationship with Jesus Christ and returned to "the world." I don't know if they returned to a physical prison, but they returned to their emotional and spiritual prisons from which they had once been set free. I know most of them had every good and honest intention to keep walking with Him, but many were powerless to resist old habits, places, and people.

Since I have been released, however, I know personally many former offenders who were transformed in prison, and who are still walking in Christ many years later. They are strong soldiers in God's army. I have seen God working in the lives of their families. I have seen them continue to prosper and experience the abundant life Jesus came to give (John 10:10). Many have their own effective ministries now. Broken relationships have been restored. Broken hearts have been healed.

What makes the difference in these two groups of people? What made the difference with me? It was clearly the "baptism in the Holy Spirit." I firmly believe that the extra level of empowerment brought about by being baptized (immersed) in the Holy Spirit makes all the difference in enabling and empowering us to walk out our faith effectively and genuinely.

When we accept the finished work of Jesus at the Cross, and confess His resurrection as the Son of God, the Holy Spirit comes to live in us. We "possess" the Spirit, and He begins His ongoing work of sanctification to steadily make our "new man" conform to the image of Christ. However, true empowerment – God's own power – comes to us, and for us, as we totally submit to the Holy Spirit and allow Him to "possess" us – one giant step more than us merely "possessing" Him inside us. We actually are able to allow Him to "possess" us!

We are baptized (immersed) into water as an outward representation of the inward change in us. We are buried with Christ in baptism (our "old man" died); and, we are raised to walk in newness of life (our "new man" came alive). But the Book of Acts makes it clear we should also desire to be baptized (immersed) into the Holy Spirit to receive the same power that resurrected Jesus from the dead – the power to walk out this new life in the way He desires for us. He in us, and us in Him!

We know the verse that says, "Greater is He that is in me than He that is in the world" (I John 4:4). So, the Holy Spirit is in us. We possess Him. But another verse we know is "I can do all things through Him who strengthens me" (Phil. 4:13). That verse is also translated as, "I can do all things through the One who empowers me within." It is the Holy Spirit that empowers us within so that we can do everything the Father desires for us to do – and assigns us to do! But we must let Him do it. We must let Him possess us.

When Jesus finished His work on earth and returned to the Father, the Father sent the Holy Spirit to earth for each of us. Jesus' followers at that time were instructed to wait until they were clothed with power from on High before they began to carry out the ministry of Jesus. We should do likewise, that is, we should seek the power of the Holy Spirit before we move out among the people in the name of Jesus. We need the power of the Holy Spirit. Within our own strength, we will burn out quickly, we will not be effective, and we can even do harm to His Kingdom.

Above all, we must remember the Holy Spirit is a person, He has a personality, and He can be grieved. His purpose in coming was to teach, lead, guide, correct, protect and comfort.... the Helper who would walk alongside us as well as dwell within us. However, we must yield to Him and allow Him to do His work in us. If we refuse Him, resist Him, or grieve Him, we will restrict the work that the Father wants Him to do in our lives. He is a gift from the Father, and we need Him!

We thank the Father for His gifts. He not only gave us His Son, Jesus, but He gave us His Holy Spirit. What a marvelous Father He is. When I think about it, I realize how gullible we are to believe the enemy's lie – the lie that the Holy Spirit is not for today, that we don't need Him. If anything, the truth is we need Him even more because we are living in the last of the last days when Scripture tells us that many will be deceived. The Holy Spirit can help us to not be deceived if we will let Him lead us and recognize that we "host" Him as the very Presence of God in us. We need Him. We need Him in His fullness.

Brothers and sisters in Christ, there are difficult times coming soon in which we will be tested. We have work He has assigned us to do. In our own strength we will fail Him, but by His power within us, working through us – His Holy Spirit – we can endure and even excel. We must stand firm to the end. We must be on our guard. Read closely what Jesus teaches in Mark 13:9-13:

"You must be on your guard. You will be handed over to the local councils and flogged in the synagogues. On account of me you will stand before governors and kings as witnesses to them. And the gospel must first be preached to all nations. Whenever you are arrested and brought to trial, do not worry beforehand about what to say Just say whatever is given you at the time, for it is not you speaking but the Holy Spirit. Brother will betray brother to death, and a father his child. Children will rebel against their parents and have them put to death. Everyone will hate you because of me, but the one who stands firm to the end will be saved."

We will not only survive, but thrive, if we have the power and discernment of the Holy Spirit. For Jesus said, "But make up your mind not to worry beforehand how you will defend yourselves. For I will give you words and wisdom that none of your adversaries will be able to resist or contradict." (Luke 21:14-15). I urge you to learn as much as possible about your Helper!

Some Relevant Scripture Passages

John 14:16-17 Jesus said, "And I will ask the Father, and he will give you another advocate to help you and be with you forever – the Spirit of truth. The world cannot accept him, because it neither sees him nor knows him. But you know him, for he lives with you and will be in you."

Acts 1:8 Jesus said, "But you will receive power when the Holy Spirit comes on you; and you will be my witnesses in Jerusalem, and in all Judea and Samaria, and to the ends of the earth."

Ephesians 3:20-21 "Now to him who is able to do immeasurably more than all we ask or imagine, according to his power that is at work within us, to him be glory in the church and in Christ Jesus throughout all generations, for ever and ever! Amen."

Colossians 1:27-29 "To them God has chosen to make known among the Gentiles the glorious riches of this mystery, which is Christ in you, the hope of glory. We proclaim him, admonishing and teaching everyone with all wisdom, so that we may present everyone perfect in Christ. To this end I labor, struggling with all his energy, which so powerfully works in me."

II Thessalonians 1:11-12 "With this in mind, we constantly pray for you, that our God may count you worthy of his calling, and that by his power he may fulfill every good purpose of yours and every act prompted by your faith. We pray this so that the name of our Lord Jesus may be glorified in you, and you in him, according to the grace of our God and the Lord Jesus Christ."

Philippians 2:11-13 "... and every tongue confess that Jesus Christ is Lord, to the glory of God the Father. Therefore, my dear friends, as you have always obeyed – not only in my presence, but now much more in my absence – continue to work out your salvation with fear and trembling, for it is God who works in you to will and to act according to his good purpose."

Galatians 2:20 "I have been crucified with Christ and I no longer live, but Christ lives in me. The life I live in the body, I live by faith in the Son of God, who loved me and gave himself for me."

John 20:21-22 "Jesus said, 'Peace be with you! As the Father has sent me, I am sending you.' And with that he breathed on them and said, 'Receive the Holy Spirit.'"

Acts 1:4-5 "On one occasion, while he was eating with them, he gave them this command: 'Do not leave Jerusalem, but wait for the gift my Father promised, which you have heard me speak about. For John baptized with water, but in a few days you will be baptized with the Holy Spirit.'"

Takeaway Highlight

Intimacy of relationship with the Father and the Son are available only through their Holy Spirit. Since the Holy Spirit is their gift to every believer to dwell inside them daily, we should learn all we can about the One Who is our Helper, Teacher, Counselor, Friend and Guide. True power to walk out the Christian life in love-motivated obedience is available only in and through the Holy Spirit.

Practical Application

Have you received the Baptism of the Holy Spirit? If you would like to ask Jesus to baptize you with fire and power, please see page 63.

Take a few minutes to really consider and appreciate the gift the Father and Son have given you! Ask the Father to help you learn to surrender more completely, daily, to the power and leadership of the Holy Spirit.

In order to be led by the Holy Spirit, we must learn to surrender daily to Him and submit to His leadership, so we are no longer regularly led by the world, the flesh and the devil. What does this look like? Read on...

SURRENDER AND SUBMISSION

An intimate personal relationship with Jesus not only requires us to surrender and repent when the Holy Spirit draws us to receive Jesus as Savior, but we must willingly submit to Jesus as Lord of our lives. We have to reach a point where we finally realize we cannot save ourselves and surrender to the only One Who can.

If we let Him, the Holy Spirit's leadership on a daily basis teaches us to make Jesus Lord of our lives and enables us to yield to His plan for our lives. We must allow Him to re-make us into the person He has always planned for us to be. As we submit to Him daily, He will show us the fullness of the abundant life Jesus came to give us (John 10:10).

The best picture of submission is one of clay in a potter's hands. The potter transforms the clay from a shapeless handful of ugly mud into an exquisite object of beautiful art. The potter is totally in charge of the transformation, and the end product is determined in large part by his patience and skill. As followers of Jesus, we can be sure we have the Master Potter!

In Isaiah 64:8 we read, "Yet, O LORD, you are our Father. We are the clay, you are the potter; we are all the work of your hand." This is illustrated in Jeremiah 18:1-6, "This is the word that came to Jeremiah from the LORD: 'Go down to the potter's house, and there I will give you my message.' So I went down to the potter's house, and I saw him working at the wheel. But the pot he was shaping from the clay was marred in his hands; so the potter formed it into another pot, shaping it as seemed best to him. Then the word of the LORD came to me: 'O house of Israel, can I not do with you as this potter does?" declares the LORD.' Like clay in the hand of the potter, so are you in my hand...'

Paul writes about the need for us to allow God to mold us as He sees fit and accept the result knowing in His wisdom He shapes us for His purpose. Romans 9:20-21 says, "But who are you, O man, to talk back to God? Shall what is formed say to him who formed it, 'Why did you make me like this?' Does not the potter have the right to make out of the same lump of clay some pottery for noble purposes and some for common use?"

Sometimes God allows extreme circumstances, like prison or other hardships of life, to get our attention. Often these may come as a consequence of poor choices made by ourselves or others, but they are best viewed as opportunities for positive change. To be transformed, a piece of clay must be soft so it will yield. We must consciously and willingly submit to God.

Regardless of how bad a mess we have made of our lives, and how far we may have run away from God, we are never so broken or so lost that God cannot find us, joyfully accept our returning to Him (Luke 15:32), make us a new creation (II Cor. 5:17) and establish His plan for our lives (Jer. 29:11-14a). However, we must be gratefully humble, prayerfully submissive and faithfully obedient. In humility we must recognize we cannot re-make ourselves and be grateful He can. In submission we must prayerfully put ourselves in His hands and patiently allow Him to form us, and subject us to the hardening fire of trials and circumstances. We must be always faithful in obedience to follow His instructions so that we will experience the best of His intentions as He accomplishes His will through us, forming us into the image of His Son (Rom. 8:29).

Pastor Adrian Rogers said, "Your fear of God should not be that He will put His hand on you, but that He will take it off."

In an article entitled "The Potter's Hands" Dr. David Jeremiah wrote, "Sometimes we think we're unusable, unredeemable. We've done something for which we feel shame and guilt, and we think God can no longer do much with us. Our problems are occasionally of our own making, and our pain arises from our own stupidity. . If you're under some sort of pressure right now, visualize the skilful hands of the divine Potter using it for good in your life... You can trust His dexterous and expert fingers not to harm, but to help you... God can take our sins and shame and spin them into a design that glorifies Him."

Dr. James MacDonald in his article, "The Potter's Wheel," asks us to "Picture a potter's wheel. The potter spins the turnstile and shapes a mound of clay into a vase, a cup, or a dish. By applying the appropriate pressure from his hands, he works the clay into a work of art. Now picture your life on that wheel. God's hand is purposeful, the pressure is the right amount in the right places. Is it sometimes painful? Almost always. Do you want to resist the process? Naturally you do. But will you trust that He will bring a good result through your being yielded to Him?"

As an ex-convict, I can relate to the term "surrender." However, in this case we surrender completely to the Lordship of Jesus, and to the Potter's hands for our benefit – in fact, for our freedom rather than our captivity or incarceration. In an article entitled "Reasons to Surrender," Dr. Charles Stanley writes, "Yielding to Him means following His way in attitude, words, thoughts, and deeds – and doing so unapologetically, unwaveringly, fearlessly."

Complete surrender and willing submission are keys to love-motivated obedience leading to an intimate personal relationship with Jesus. Have you truly surrendered to the Hands of our Potter?

Some Relevant Scripture Passages

John 10:10 Jesus said, "The thief comes only to steal and kill and destroy; I have come that they may have life, and have it to the full."

Romans 8:28-29 "And we know that in all things God works for the good of those who love him, who have been called according to his purpose. For those God foreknew he also predestined to be conformed to the image of his Son, that he might be the firstborn among many brothers and sisters."

Jeremiah 29:11-14 "For I know the plans I have for you," declares the Lord, "plans to prosper you and not to harm you, plans to give you hope and a future. Then you will call on me and come and pray to me, and I will listen to you. You will seek me and find me when you seek me with all your heart. I will be found by you," declares the Lord, "and will bring you back from captivity. I will gather you from all the nations and places where I have banished you," declares the Lord, "and will bring you back to the place from which I carried you into exile."

Romans 9:20-21 "But who are you, a human being, to talk back to God? Shall what is formed say to the one who formed it, 'Why did you make me like this?' Does not the potter have the right to make out of the same lump of clay some pottery for special purposes and some for common use?"

Isaiah 64:8 "Yet you, Lord, are our Father. We are the clay, you are the potter; we are all the work of your hand."

Jeremiah 18:1-6 "This is the word that came to Jeremiah from the Lord: 'Go down to the potter's house, and there I will give you my message.' So I went down to the potter's house, and I saw him working at the wheel. But the pot he was shaping from the clay was marred in his hands; so the potter formed it into another pot, shaping it as seemed best to him. Then the word of the Lord came to me. He said, 'Can I not do with you, Israel, as this potter does?' declares the Lord. Like clay in the hand of the potter, so are you in my hand, Israel.'"

Takeaway Highlight

Complete surrender and willing submission are keys to love-motivated obedience leading to an intimate personal relationship with Jesus.

Practical Application

Spend some time thinking about the fact that our Father God already sees in His mind's eye what He wants to make of you. He already knows the full, perfect and complete plan He desires for you. Will you let Him have His way completely, or will you hold back? Tell Him you trust Him enough to be patient during the progression of His creative work in you. Your intimacy of relationship is directly related to how much you willingly surrender and submit.

An intimate relationship with Jesus starts the minute we repent, surrender, believe the Gospel, and are born again. Proof of our love for Him is revealed in our obedience...

PRINCIPLES OF OBEDIENCE

The more we believe and receive God's love for us, the more we will be motivated by that love to be obedient. One of our dear prison ministers and close friend, Carol Breeden, graduated to Heaven in 2020. Here is something she wrote on obedience that seems especially relevant to our goal of pursuing an intimacy of personal relationship with Jesus:

"This may not be your favorite subject; however, I have found that the more I walk in obedience to His Word, the more peaceful my life is. You see, there was a time in my life when I would read His Word but didn't understand it. So many times when I made daily choices, those choices would be against His Word and I was not even aware of my disobedience. That is very displeasing to God. Not only was God displeased, but I suffered the consequences of my wrong choices, not even understanding what was happening. That, my friend, is like looking into a mirror at myself, and then turning away and forgetting what I looked like.

"So it is important that we study His Word, and it is important that we understand it. How can we be a 'doer' of His Word if we do not understand what His Word means? God has a beautiful plan for each of us, and He shares in His Word what He expects from us. The more I understand His plan, the more grateful I become. And the more grateful I become, the more I love Him. And the more I love Him, the more I want to walk in obedience.

"Our heavenly Father loves us. He doesn't want us to follow a list of 'do's and don'ts' out of fear for what will happen if we don't. He wants us to love Him in return. And because we love Him, we walk in obedience to His Word. If you have children, would you want them to be afraid of you? Would you want them to obey you out of fear? No, I believe you would want them to obey you because they love you and they realize that you are looking out for their best interests – that you are making decisions on their behalf based on what you think is best for them. That is what our Father has done, you know. He has set principles into motion for our protection. When we obey those principles, it will be well with our souls!

"God does not want us to just go through the motions of loving Him. He wants genuine love. We can sometimes pretend with our friends' to care for them just so we can get from them what we want. But that is not a loving relationship, and it will soon turn sour. Likewise, your heavenly Father knows what is in your heart. Do you know what is in your heart? Do you really love Him? Jesus said, 'If you love me, then keep My commandments.' Obedience is better than sacrifice."

As I thought about this phrase, "obedience is better than sacrifice" (see 1 Samuel 15:22), it occurs to me to emphasize that man-made religious rituals are not effective. What honors God is a heart that is set on obeying Him, and is quick to repent when we miss the mark in rebellion.

Blessings Follow Obedience

When I was released from prison, Freedom in Jesus Ministries' Founder, Don Castleberry, began mentoring me about our Christian journey – a journey leading to the very presence of God. We can experience His Presence in this life. We do not have to die first. But in the process, God never advances us any further than our last act of disobedience. Think about this – His best for us lies on the other side of our obedience.

A.W. Tozer, in *Experiencing the Presence of God*, wrote, "Which is more important to a Christian, believing or obeying? For the sparrow flying through the air, both wings are equally important. With only one it is impossible to fly. So we must believe God's Word and obey it. By these two wings, a man will rise to God in faith and humble obedience to the Lord Himself...very few Christians are prepared to go with God all the way. They go part of the way and then improvise. They follow the Lord until things look a little sticky and then they say, 'Well, there's no use to get radical about this and be a fanatic. I think I can reason this out for myself.'...The result is, of course, luke-warmness, which God will spew out of His mouth."

David Wilkerson wrote, "No matter who you are, if you harbor a secret sin you will experience continual disturbances in your life, your home and family, your work. Confusion, worry, and fears will replace your peace and strength."

I remember times in the past when I needed God to do something, and I thought I was waiting on Him. I learned, however, that He was waiting on me! Waiting for what? He wanted first my obedience in a certain area of my life I had been selfishly withholding. Once I surrendered that area to Him, His blessings were released, and I experienced more of His Presence daily.

In a devotional, *100 Days of Prayer for a Righteous Man*, I read, "Are you ready, willing, able, and anxious to receive God's blessings? Then obey Him. And you can rest assured that when you do your part, He'll do His part!"

Ask the Holy Spirit to show you any areas in which you are not presently obedient. Then surrender them fully to God. His blessings are waiting for you!

'Only he who believes is obedient, and only he who is obedient believes." Dietrich Bonhoeffer

Some Relevant Scripture Passages

Micah 6:8 – "He has shown you, O mortal, what is good. And what does the Lord require of you? To act justly and to love mercy and to walk humbly with your God."

Joshua 22:5 – "But be very careful to keep the commandment and the law that Moses the servant of the Lord gave you: to love the Lord your God, to walk in obedience to him, to keep his commands, to hold fast to him and to serve him with all your heart and with all your soul."

John 14:23 "Jesus replied, 'If anyone loves me, he will obey my teaching. My Father will love him, and we will come to him and make our home with him.'"

I John 5:2-4 "This is how we know that we love the children of God: by loving God and carrying out his commands. This is love for God: to obey his commands. And his commands are not burdensome, for everyone born of God overcomes the world. This is the victory that has overcome the world, even our faith."

Proverbs 13:13 "He who scorns instruction will pay for it, but he who respects a command is rewarded."

I John 2:17 "The world and its desires pass away, but the man who does the will of God lives forever."

Deuteronomy 26:16-19 "The LORD your God commands you this day to follow these decrees and laws; carefully observe them with all your heart and with all your soul. You have declared this day that the LORD is your God and that you will walk in his ways, that you will keep his decrees, commands and laws, and that you will obey him. And the LORD has declared this day that you are his people, his treasured possession as he promised, and that you are to keep all his commands. He has declared that he will set you in praise, fame and honor high above all the nations he has made and that you will be a people holy to the LORD your God, as he promised."

John 15:14 – "Jesus said, 'You are my friends if you do what I command.'"

John 14:15 – "Jesus said, 'If you love me, keep my commands.'"

I John 3:24 – "The one who keeps God's commands lives in him, and he in them. And this is how we know that he lives in us: We know it by the Spirit he gave us."

I John 2:3-4 – "We know that we have come to know him if we keep his commands. Whoever says, 'I know him,' but does not do what he commands is a liar, and the truth is not in that person."

I John 5:2-3 – "This is how we know that we love the children of God: by loving God and carrying out his commands. In fact, this is love for God: to keep his commands. And his commands are not burdensome."

Titus 1:16 – "They claim to know God, but by their actions they deny him. They are detestable, disobedient and unfit for doing anything good."

Deuteronomy 28:1-14 – "If you fully obey the LORD your God and carefully follow all his commands I give you today, the LORD your God will set you high above all the nations on earth. All these blessings will come upon you and accompany you if you obey the LORD your God: You will be blessed in the city and blessed in the country. The fruit of your womb will be blessed, and the crops of your land and the young of your livestock – the calves of your herds and the lambs of your flocks. Your basket and your kneading trough will be blessed. You will be blessed when you come in and blessed when you go out. The LORD will grant that the enemies who rise up against you will be defeated before you. They will come at you from one direction but flee from you in seven. The LORD will send a blessing on your barns and on everything you put your hand to. The LORD your God will bless you in the land he is giving you. The LORD will establish you as his holy people, as he promised you on oath, if you keep the commands of the LORD your God and walk in his ways. Then all the peoples on earth will see that you are called by the name of the LORD, and they will fear you. The LORD will grant you abundant prosperity – in the fruit of your womb, the young of your livestock and the crops of your ground – in the land he swore to your forefathers to give you. The LORD will open the heavens, the storehouse of his bounty, to send rain on your land in season and to bless all the work of your hands. You will lend to many nations but will borrow from none. The LORD will make you the head, not the tail. If you pay attention to the commands of the LORD your God that I give you this day and carefully follow them, you will always be at the top, never at the bottom. Do not turn aside from any of the commands I give you today, to the right or to the left, following other gods and serving them."

Takeaway Highlight

A.W. Tozer, in *Experiencing the Presence of God*, wrote, "Which is more important to a Christian, believing or obeying? For the sparrow flying through the air, both wings are equally important. With only one it is impossible to fly. So we must believe God's Word and obey it. By these two wings, a man will rise to God in faith and humble obedience to the Lord Himself."

Practical Application

Prayerfully consider any areas in your life where you are not being obedient. Ask the Holy Spirit to bring these to mind. He will not do it to condemn you (Romans 8:1) but to gently convict you of righteousness (John 16:8-11). In your Christian journey do you feel stuck, unable to move forward? The areas of disobedience brought to your mind by the Holy Spirit may be your roadblocks. God wants you to deal with them, fully surrender, and move forward. Trust Him.

Final Question

After considering all the information presented in this booklet, have you been born again?

If not, or if you are uncertain, talk to God about your desire and willingness to make a commitment to Him. He will never force you to serve Him or seek Him.

The next steps are up to you...

TRANSFORMATION ILLUSTRATION

The "Old Man"
Six Months Before Prison (2007)
Stephen Canup

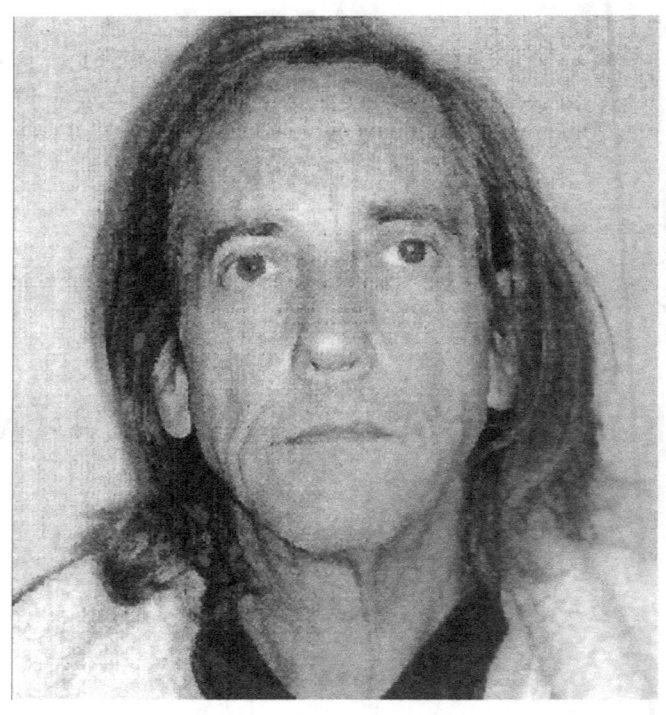

Guilty and Condemned by Sin to Death
Romans 6:23 "For the wages of sin is death..."

GUILTY OF THESE SINS AGAINST GOD, OTHERS AND SELF:

Addictions to drugs, alcohol, sex, pornography, praise of men, work

Pride	Judgment	Thievery
Worry	Self-hate	Adultery
Fear	Resentment	Sexual identity
Depression	Regret	Confusion
Hopelessness	Anger	Lying
Anxiety	Covetousness	Conceit
Profanity	Depravity	Intellectualism
Fornication	Reprobation	Humanism
Lustful desires	Un-forgiveness	Shame
Perversion	Immorality	Remorse
Idolatry	Self-abuse	Guilt
Selfishness	Bitterness	Offense

THE SINFUL AND CURSED LIFE I WAS LIVING BEFORE PRISON RESULTED IN ME BEING:

- Homeless, living on the streets of Nashville, TN, for 3 years prior to prison.
- Unemployed for 7 years prior to incarceration.
- Broke after having filed for bankruptcy twice.
- Destitute with all my earthly possessions contained in 1 hanging garment bag in the prison's property room awaiting the day of my release.
- Desolate having abandoned all family and friends, leaving me lonely and utterly forsaken.
- Depressed so deeply by these life conditions that I had attempted suicide several times.
- Hopeless and absolutely convinced nothing would ever change or get better in any way.

The "New Man"
One Year After Prison (2012)
Stephen Canup

A Free Man – Alive in Christ

...but the gift of God is eternal life in Christ Jesus our Lord." Romans 6:23

"I have been crucified with Christ and I no longer live, but Christ lives in me. The life I now live in the body, I live by faith in the Son of God, who loved me and gave himself for me." (Gal. 2:20)

"Therefore if any is (ingrafted) in Christ, the Messiah, he is (a new creature altogether), a new creation; the old (previous moral and spiritual condition) has passed away. Behold, the fresh and new has come!"
(II Cor. 5:17, AMP)

"So if the Son sets you free, you will be free indeed"
(John 8:36)

The new life in Christ that began in prison in 2009 has brought many blessings. As of early 2024, some of these abundant life realities include:

- My spiritual re-birth April 20, 2009!!!
- Restored relationships with every family member.
- A mentor and accountability partner, Don Castleberry, who speaks the truth in love.
- Acceptance instead of rejection.
- Joy and hope instead of depression and hopelessness.
- Purpose and passion to help set others free.
- Peace, boldness and confidence instead of anxiety and fear.
- The righteousness of Christ Jesus instead of perversion and depravity.
- Love and compassion for others instead of selfishness and self-hate.
- Freedom from addictions to alcohol, drugs, pornography, smoking and gambling.
- A tongue of blessings and respect instead of pride, criticism and profanity.
- A beautiful, three bedroom, two bath home provided rent-free except for utilities.

- Three late-model vehicles have been provided to me free, in great condition, with low mileage.
- A house full of good furniture, and a closet full of good clothes.
- Debt-free, with also some money in savings.
- A renewed mind free of all the bad effects of addictions and depression.
- Good health.
- Mature Christians I can call for prayer or advice anytime about anything.
- Licensed and ordained in 2012 as a minister of the Gospel of Jesus Christ.
- President of Freedom in Jesus Prison Ministries.
- Author of eight books to encourage the body of Christ behind razor wire.

TAKE ACTION

YOU CAN HAVE "THE REAL THING"

"The Real Thing" has nothing to do with religion.

Rather, it is an intimate personal relationship with our Heavenly Father, because of the finished work of Jesus at the Cross. The Holy Spirit comes and seals us as His very own, and begins an ongoing work in us to conform us to the image of Christ Jesus.

You can begin this exciting and abundant life today. It will continue throughout all eternity.

First, acknowledge and confess that you have sinned against God.

Second, renounce your sins – determine that you are not going back to them.

Third, by faith receive Christ into your heart. Surrender your life completely to Him. He will come to live in your heart by the Holy Spirit.

You can do this right now.

Start by simply talking to God. You can pray a prayer like this:

"Oh God, I am a sinner. I'm sorry for my sin. I want to turn from my sin. Please forgive me. I believe Jesus Christ is Your Son; I believe He died on the Cross for my sin and You raised Him to life. I want to trust Him as my Savior and follow Him as my Lord from this day forward, forevermore. Lord Jesus, I put my trust in You and surrender my life to You. Please come into my life and fill me with your Holy Spirit. In Jesus' Name. Amen."

If you just said this prayer, and you meant it with all your heart, we believe you were just Saved and are now Born Again in Christ Jesus as a totally new person.

"Therefore, if anyone is in Christ, he is a new creation; the old has gone, the new has come!"

We urge you to go "all in and all out for the All in All"! (Pastor Mark Batterson, All In)

We suggest you follow the Lord in water baptism at your earliest opportunity. Water baptism is an outward symbol of the inward change that follows your salvation and re-birth.

The grace of God Himself gives you the desire and ability to surrender completely to the Holy Spirit's work in and through you (Philippians 2:13).

The Baptism in the Holy Spirit is His empowerment for you.

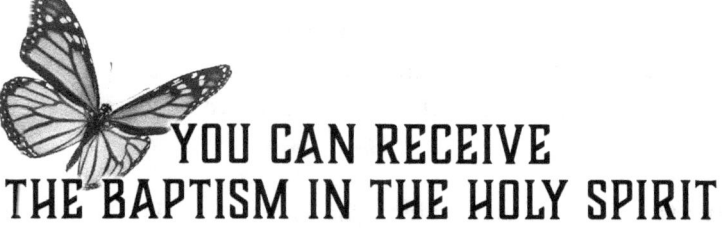

YOU CAN RECEIVE THE BAPTISM IN THE HOLY SPIRIT

The Baptism in the Holy Spirit is a separate experience and a Holy privilege granted to those who ask. This is God's own power to enable you to live an abundant, overcoming life. The Bible says it is the same power that raised Jesus from the dead.

Have you asked the Father for Jesus to baptize you (immerse you) in the Holy Spirit (Luke 3:16)? If you ask the Father, He will give Him to you (Luke 11:13). Have you allowed the "rivers of living water" to flow from within you (John 7:38-39)? Our Father desires for us to walk in all His fullness by His Holy Spirit.

The power to witness and live your life the way Jesus did in intimate relationship with the Father, comes from asking Jesus to baptize you in the Holy Spirit. To receive this baptism, pray along these lines:

Abba Father and my Lord Jesus,

Thank you for giving me your Spirit to live inside me. I am saved by grace through faith in Jesus. I ask you now to baptize me in the Holy Ghost with Your fire and power. I fully receive it through faith just like I did my salvation. Now, Holy Spirit, come and rise up within me as I praise God! Fill me up Jesus! I fully expect to receive my prayer language as You give me utterance. In Jesus' Name. Amen.

Now, out loud, begin to praise and glorify JESUS, because He is the baptizer of the Holy Spirit! From deep in your spirit, tell Him, "I love you, I thank you, I praise you, Jesus."

Repeat this as you feel joy and gratefulness bubble up from deep inside you. Speak those words and syllables you receive – not in your own language, but the language given to you by the Holy Spirit. Allow this joy to come out of you in syllables of a language your own mind does not know. That will be your prayer language the Spirit will use through you when you don't know how to pray (Romans 8:26-28). It is not the "gift of tongues" for public use, therefore it does not require a public interpretation.

You have to use your own voice. The Holy Spirit is a gentleman. He will not force you to speak. Don't be concerned with how it sounds. It is a heavenly language!

Worship Him! Praise Him! Use your heavenly language by praying in the Spirit every day! Paul urges us to "pray in the Spirit on all occasions with all kinds of prayers and requests." (Ephesians 6:18)

Your heavenly language of tongues for prayer might not come immediately. It is only one evidence of the Baptism in the Holy Spirit. Some others are: a hunger for the Word of God; a thirst for righteousness; a desire for sanctification and a daily surrender to the leading of the Holy Spirit.

Draw near to God daily. He will draw near to you (James 4:8)

WATER BAPTISM

After receiving the finished work of Jesus at the Cross and being "born again," you will want to commit to Jesus as the Lord of your life. He commanded his disciples to baptize new followers.

"Then Jesus came to them and said, 'All authority in heaven and on earth has been given to me. Therefore go and make disciples of all nations, baptizing them in the name of the Father and of the Son and of the Holy Spirit, and teaching them to obey everything I have commanded you. And surely I am with you always, to the very end of the age.'" Matthew 28:18-20

The Lord commands all believers to be baptized as a means of identifying with Him. Baptism is for the saved – the act itself does not save us. Rather, it is the first public act of obedience done by a new Christian. Water baptism is our way of making a visible, public declaration that we have determined to depart from our former lifestyle and obey God's Word.

Baptism is not an option for New Testament believers. It is the first step we can take in order to show our allegiance to the Lord. It portrays our identification with the death, burial, and resurrection of the Lord Jesus. It is our means of identifying with His purpose, and demonstrating to others that we are yielding our life to the guidance of the Son. It also identifies us with other believers who are the body of Christ.

Baptism by immersion in water is also a picture of what has happened to us – we have died to an old way of life and have been raised to live a new life. It says to all who observe, "I have renounced all of self, I have died to self, and I am now alive, living my life for Jesus Christ. I identify with Him! I am not ashamed of Him. I have been overwhelmed completely by Him!" You see, for a few seconds while you are under the water, you are as if dead, then you are raised up alive to walk in the newness of Jesus Christ. It is a picture of regeneration that has already taken place in your soul (Romans 6:3-5).

The truly saved and baptized person shows by his new life that his old nature, his human nature, has been put in the place of death. Baptism is an outward ceremony which is useless unless the old nature is looked upon as dead and the new life is allowed to live (II Corinthians 5:17).

We encourage you to be baptized at your earliest opportunity. Ask your Pastor or Chaplain when the next Baptism Service will be.

I CHALLENGE YOU!!!

God is able to transform your life in the same way He did mine. Understanding and receiving God's love is key; and willing obedience is necessary.

But you must understand that He rewards those who diligently and earnestly seek Him (Hebrews 11:6); and, that you are transformed by renewing your mind through applying the principles in His Word to your daily life (Romans 12:1-2).

I challenge you to:

Start every day with the Word and the Spirit. Ask the Holy Spirit to help you apply His Truth to your life. Let the Spirit use the Word to transform you.

Look up every scripture reference in this book. Mark the verses in your own Bible. Memorize the ones that mean the most to you.

Study the scriptural principles in this book in small groups. Sharing concepts from the Word with others helps you learn and apply them to your life.

Show this book to others. As an ambassador for Christ (see 2 Corinthians 5:18-20), please use this book as a tool to reach the lost and encourage the Body of Believers.

Please pray daily for us and for our ministry. We need your prayers.

Ask your loved ones to check out our ministry website at www.fijm.org.

They can learn more about Stephen Canup's books at www.stephencanup.com

Do you want to help us continue to provide books like these free to prisoners? At your first opportunity, begin a program of regular giving to us so we can better minister to others who want to be free from every form of bondage. Former prisoners helping prisoners is what we are all about.

We pray you are blessed abundantly by our Father every day, in every way, in Christ Jesus as you seek Him daily in and by the Holy Spirit!

MY PERSONAL FAITH JOURNEY

MY PERSONAL FAITH JOURNEY

MY PERSONAL FAITH JOURNEY

MY PERSONAL FAITH JOURNEY

Rescue, Redemption, and Relationship

ALL BOOKS AVAILABLE AT WWW.FIJM.ORG

Devotion and Discipleship

After being on top of the world with a CPA office on Park Avenue, Stephen Canup lost it all and found himself homeless and incarcerated. *Jail-House Religion* is his true life story on God's redeeming love and grace.

Stephen's second book, *Diving Deeper*, is a daily discipleship field guide that encourages and challenges the reader into a more abundant life of freedom and renewal.

Ex-convicts and felons in general, and former sex offenders in particular, are treated as modern day lepers. *Lepers No More* illustrates how society's outcasts are healed and restored.

Knowing God Series

Thinking about establishing a relationship with God can be intimidating. However, seeking and maintaining one with each of the three persons of the Godhead is achievable—Father, Son, and Holy Spirit! Learn how in this series.

These books are available at the Freedom in Jesus website www.fijm.org for friends and family to purchase for themselves or for someone they love. (Shipping into a correctional facility is available.)

Preview books at www.stephencanup.com

IN JESUS
PRISON MINISTRIES

STEPHEN CANUP

AND

FREEDOM IN JESUS PRISON MINISTRIES

HEARTILY RECOMMENDS

KINGDOM TOWERS

LUBBOCK, TX

AS A GREAT PLACE TO START OVER!

www.ingramcontent.com/pod-product-compliance
Lightning Source LLC
Chambersburg PA
CBHW072133070526
44585CB00016B/1658